Dum

101 Fast, Healthy and Easy Dump Dinner Recipes for Everyone

By:

J.J. Lewis

Want more Bestseller Cook Books for FREE?

Join my **V.I.P** Reading List where I give away **Healthy** and Delicious Recipes FOR **FREE!**

Yes, you heard me right! COMPLETELY FREE to everyone just for being a loyal reader of mine!

http://www.mritchi.com/freecookbook

Copyright © 2015 by Ravens Press
All rights reserved. This book or any portion thereof
may not be reproduced or used in any manner whatsoever
without the express written permission of the publisher
except for the use of brief quotations in a book review.

ISBN-13: 978-1512166194

ISBN-10: 1512166197

www.amazon.com/author/jjlewis

Table of Contents

Introduction 1

1. Lemon & Garlic Chicken 4
2. Crock Pot Apricot Chicken 4
3. Easy Cheesy Chicken Casserole 5
4. Mexican Chicken Lasagna 6
5. Baked Chicken Taquitos 7
6. Sweet Potatoes Pesto 9
7. Barbecued Meatball Dinner 10
8. Chicken with pesto butter 11
9. Philly Cheese steak 12
10. Cheese and Shrimp Chowder 13
11. Creole Dump Chicken 14
12. Fisherman Stew 15
13. Russian Chicken 16
14. Parisienne Chicken 17
15. Potato Chicken 18
16. Spicy Chicken Legs 19
17. Meatballs 20
18. Sticky Turkey 21
19. Teriyaki Dump Chicken 21
20. Spiced-Citrus Chicken 23
21. Macho Nacho Chicken 24
22. Tipsy Chicken 24
23. Creole Chicken 25
24. Chicken & Noodles 27
25. Delicious Chicken 27
26. Super Chicken 28
27. Chicken wings 29
28. Slow Cooker Dump and Go Cheesy Chicken 30
29. Dump Casserole 31

30.	Chinese Pork & Vegetable Hot Pot	32
31.	Slow-cooker massaman lamb shanks	33
32.	Italian Beef	34
33.	Sour Cream Roast	35
34.	Dump Coke	37
35.	Lemon Dill "dump" Chicken	38
36.	Dump Pepper Lime Chicken	39
37.	Pineapple dump Chicken	40
38.	Sweet Salsa Dump Chicken	41
39.	Dump Swiss steak	42
40.	Grandma Randolph's Noodles	43
41.	Super Quick Dump Pot Roast	44
42.	Teriyaki Chicken Crockpot	45
43.	Dump It in Meatloaf	46
44.	Lemon Garlic Dump Chicken	47
45.	Pineapple-Honey lamb chops	48
46.	Fruity Crock Pot Chicken	49
47.	Apricot Chicken	50
48.	Shredded Beef Burritos	51
49.	Machaca Beef	53
50.	Cube Steak and Gravy	54
51.	Beef Stroganoff	55
52.	Honey Glazed "dump" Chicken	56
53.	Thunderbird Roast	57
54.	Turkey Breast	58
55.	Slow Cooker Taco Soup	59
56.	Crunch Cherry Dump Cake	60
57.	Fruit Dump Cake	62
58.	Pumpkin Dump Cake	63
59.	Peach Cobbler Dump Cake	64
60.	Blueberry Dump Cake	65

61.	Black Forest Dump Cake	66
62.	Three-Fruit Dump Cake	67
63.	Beef Fajitas	68
64.	Beef Stroganoff	70
65.	Pot Roast	71
66.	Ham and Broccoli Casserole	71
67.	Shrimp and Cheese Chowder	72
68.	Italian Style Eggplant	74
69.	Beef Roast Sandwich with Au Jus Dip	75
70.	Meat Loaf	76
71.	Chicken Teriyaki	77
72.	Goulash	78
73.	Cuban Beans	79
74.	Potato and Ham Casserole	81
75.	Beans and Corn Chicken Dinner	82
76.	Mixed Vegetable Curry	83
77.	Meatballs with Sweet and Sour Sauce	84
78.	Chicken Adobo	85
79.	Barbecued Pot Roast	86
80.	Chicken Cacciatore	87
81.	Dump Chicken Caribbean Style	88
82.	Vegetable and Beef Soup	89
83.	Shrimp and Cheese Chowder	90
84.	Chicken with Sweet Salsa	92
85.	Clam Chowder	93
86.	Chicken Taco Soup	94
87.	Chicken and Shrimp Jambalaya	95
88.	Curried Pork over Rice	96
89.	Char Siew Pork	98
90.	Roast Turkey Mediterranean Style	99
91.	Flaxseed Oatmeal	100

92.	Oysters	101
93.	Kale Chips	102
94.	Beef and Vegetable Soup	104
95.	Lentil Soup	105
96.	Pumpkin Soup	106
97.	Pepperoncini Beef	107
98.	Cinnamon And Apple With Oats	108
99.	Breakfast Quinoa	109
100.	Spinach and Mushroom Quiche	110
101.	Cranberry Punch	111

Conclusion 113

Introduction

Are you like most families who rely on pizza, burger or takeout dinners? Or maybe the type that resorts to processed foods from the frozen section, only to reheat bland and nutrient-lacking cardboard dishes in the microwave to serve to your family? I feel you. Like most average families nowadays, we are too busy with our personal life, career, making ends meet, family life and whatever else distracts us to caring for ourselves that making dinner takes the backseat in our lives. But, this shouldn't be so.

We all know the repercussions of always buying fast foods; it's high in calories but empty in nutrients plus all sorts of preservatives to make the food palatable. What about those frozen burritos? It is cheap but it's not fresh food. It's still laced with preservatives that are not good for you.

I really understand your thoughts on the effort of cooking dinner and this is where I teach you the perks of Dump Dinners! Pair it with your slow cooker and cooking dinner is a cinch. You can prepare your crockpot dump dinner early in the morning before you go to work or bring the kids to school, let it cook on slow for 8 hours or more and by the time you get back in the afternoon from work, from fetching the kids in school your dinner is ready. That's how easy it is. Wait, you say? What about the preparation for the food? I don't have that much energy, cooking skills or the time to prepare much. Well, the preparation time is around 15 minutes. Since, you will be using fresh ingredients, there may be a bit of chopping and washing needed then dump everything into the crockpot and you are good to go.

You just need a moment to prepare the dump recipes and believe me these recipes are amazingly quick and very easy recipes. With Dump Recipes, you can still give your loved ones all those minerals and vitamins that were present inside the raw food.

Despite the fact that you go about your busy life; simply dump the recipes into your Crockpot, let them cook and enjoy delicious meals or desserts, you could ever have. Most of the dump recipes involve mixing up the ingredients and just popping them into a Crockpot (slow cooker) for a set number of hours.

Getting your dinner placed on the table every night could really be a difficult task as we all live in a really busy world. When you're short of time and schedules are hectic, you may try and consider the dump recipes for you and your loved ones. These dinner recipes are very simple and are as easy as mix and go.

Just after coming home from your work, the last thing you ever wish to perform is spending an hour in the kitchen. Thankfully with the help of dump dinners, these are the things of the past. Let your Slow Cooker do the work on your behalf and don't consider yourself to be a slave in the Kitchen. You may spend the time that you were supposed to spend in the kitchen with your children or anyone you like.

You need not have to spend the entire day in the kitchen and doing the stuff like chopping, stirring and cooking. Dump recipes not only save your valuable time but they are delicious too.

 A few minutes of preparation then set and forget about it. Come home to the mouth-watering smell of your already cooked dinner, just waiting for you to simply serve it up to your hungry loved ones.

 Doesn't matter if they're quick skillet meals that cook up in record time or they're easy slow cooker recipes that simmer entire day at the same time as you go about your business, any one of these dinner ideas would surely save the day for you.

If you talk about a busy weeknight then who doesn't love an appetizing slow cooker chicken recipe in the dinner? The dump recipes are the easiest dinner recipes that you'll ever make and believe me these recipes are so delicious that you would never believe on.

Of course, nothing this good is for free. You have to make a bit of a commitment and take a few minutes from your busy schedule to make. But the benefits that you provide your family and yourself cannot be stressed enough and is priceless!

1. Lemon & Garlic Chicken

Ingredients:

8 to 10 chicken tenders (or 4 to 6 chicken breasts)

2 tbsp. of lemon juice (or you may extract the juice from a lemon)

1 tbsp. of parsley flakes

1 to 2 tsp. of garlic, minced (depends on your taste)

1/4 c. of olive oil

Preparation:

Place all the ingredients into a freezer bag (probably 1-gallon). Once you seal the bag, turn the bag over more than a few times until the chicken is well coated and everything is combined. Freeze flat.

Directions:

1. Place the frozen chicken in the Crockpot, cook on high approximately for 4 to 6 hrs. (Or on low for 6 to 8 hrs.) until the chicken is cooked and no longer pink inside.

OR

1. Defrost the chicken first then transfer the chicken and marinade into a baking dish, to coat the chicken, turn it several times. Bake at 175 C/350 F approximately for 35 minutes.

2. Crock Pot Apricot Chicken

Ingredients:

3 pounds chicken pieces, skinless

1/2 c. of Apricot jam

1/2 c. of French dressing

1 packet onion soup mix, dry (1.5 oz.)

Directions:

1. Whisk together soup mix, jam and dressing in a bowl.
2. Brush every section of the chicken with sauce; place the chicken in the Crockpot. Cover the chicken with any leftover sauce.
3. Cover and cook on high approximately for 3 to 4 hrs. or on Low approximately for 6 to 8 hrs.

3. Easy Cheesy Chicken Casserole

Ingredients

16 ounce cooked egg noodles

1 (14 ounce) can chicken or 3 to 4 chicken breasts (chopped and cooked)

2 cans cream of chicken soup

24 ounce sour cream

8 ounce mozzarella cheese, shredded

8 ounce cheddar cheese, shredded

1/4 c. of melted margarine

1 sleeve Ritz crackers, crushed

2 Tbsp. of Poppy seeds (optional)

Directions:

1. In a large bowl, combine sour cream, chicken, cheeses & soup; stir to combine. Now put in the noodles, stir gently till well coated.
2. Transfer the ingredients into a greased baking dish (9×13). Mix margarine and crackers and sprinkle over the top.
3. Sprinkle with the Poppy seeds. Bake at 175 C/350 F degrees approximately for half an hour or till cheese is melted and crackers are golden brown and crispy.

4.   Mexican Chicken Lasagna

Ingredients:

1 can cream of each chicken and mushroom soup

3 to 4 c. of chicken, chopped and cooked

1 can tomatoes, mild Ro-Tel

1 c. of frozen corn nib lets (you may even use canned, drained)

1 can fiesta nacho cheese

4 large, burrito style flour tortillas

2 c. of Mexican cheese blend, shredded

1 can black beans, rinsed

1/4 c. of cilantro, fresh and chopped

For garnish:

Lime wedges

Fresh cilantro

Chopped tomatoes

Pickled jalapeno slices

Sour cream

Directions:

1. Preheat the oven to 175 C/350 F. Mix together cooked chicken, chicken and mushroom soup, nacho cheese, Ro-Tel tomatoes and fresh cilantro.
2. Add 1 c. of the filling into a casserole dish all set with the cooking spray and simply start layering all the ingredients.
3. Now with aluminum foil, cover it loosely. Make sure that the cheese should not touch the foil. Bake covered approximately for 20 minutes at 175 C/350 F, then uncovered until heated all the way through or approximately for 10 minutes (Remember- it would take longer to heat through, if you refrigerated it and made this ahead of time).
4. Top it with your favorite garnishes such as slices pickled jalapenos, grape tomatoes and fresh cilantro. Just before serving, add some flavors like lime wedges and sour cream on the side.

5. **Baked Chicken Taquitos**

Ingredients:

1 pack of egg roll wrappers

Rotisserie chicken – completely cooked, seasoned.

1 c. of "Mexican blend" cheese, shredded

2/3 to 1 c. of fresh salsa or jarred

1/3 c. of black beans, canned, drained and rinsed

Large pinch of cilantro, fresh and chopped

1/3 c. of sweet yellow and white corn nib lets

1 tsp. of ground cumin

Pepper and salt

Directions:

1. From the rotisserie chicken simply remove the chicken and chop the chicken into small pieces (bite-sized).
2. Mix all the ingredients (except fresh cilantro and egg roll wrapper) into the chicken and combine well.
3. Add some spoonful's of the chicken mixture to the eggroll wrapper. First fold in the sides and then roll. With water, wet the far end so that it would stick itself.
4. With butter flavored spray (nonstick), spray a cookie sheet and put together the taquitos. With the butter flavored spray, spray the tops of the taquitos and sprinkle them with extra cumin and black pepper.
5. Bake at 175 C/375 F until golden brown or approximately for 25 minutes. If you can remember, you may turn them onto their

sides. Serve with your favorites condiments like salsa, light sour cream etc.

6. Sweet Potatoes Pesto

Ingredients

1 sweet potato poked with a fork

3 eggs cooked

For the pesto

1 garlic clove, peeled

⅔ c. of walnuts

½ lemon's juice

1-1.5 c. basil leaves (fresh)

salt and pepper according to taste

½ c. olive oil

Directions:

1) Take a fork and make holes in the potato then wrap it in a foil and place in a Crockpot approximately for 4 hrs. on high or 8 hrs. on low heat. In case you want to cook it faster, heat the sweet potato in the Microwave at 218 C/425 F approximately for 20-25 minutes.

2) Remove the potato from the foil and let it cool (once the potato is cooked), before removing the skin. Then take a fork and crush the sweet potato.

3) For the pesto, put walnuts in a food processor along with garlic clove, basil leaves and pulse until the leaves are break down. While the food processor is still running add the olive oil slowly. Lastly, add lemon juice and a bit of pepper and salt (according to your taste). Puree it until smooth.

4) Once pesto is finished mix 2 to 5 tbsp. of the pesto into the mashed potato.

5) The next step would be to cook an egg. Just before serving, add egg on top of sweet potato pesto mash.

7. Barbecued Meatball Dinner

Ingredients:

1 package meatballs, frozen

For the Sauce:

1 c. of packed brown sugar

1 c. ketchup

6 ounce tomato paste

1/4 c. of cider vinegar

1/4 c. soy sauce, reduced-sodium

1 or more tsp. of hot pepper sauce (as per your taste)

Directions:

1. Combine brown sugar, ketchup, soy sauce, tomato paste, hot pepper sauce and vinegar, mixing well in a medium bowl. Dump

the meatballs into the slow cooker. Pour the sauce over the meatballs. Cover, cook on low approximately for 4 to 5 hrs.
2. Just before serving this recipe, place a heap of hot cooked (Brown rice or Jasmine) in the middle of the plate and then put in the meatballs. Serve with a steamed veggie or side salad.

8. Chicken with pesto butter

Ingredients:

1.6kg whole chicken

2 tbsp. of basil, cashew and parmesan dip

60g butter, softened

2 tbsp. of chopped fresh basil leaves

1 tbsp. of olive oil

Steamed broccoli, beans and carrots, to serve

1 garlic clove, finely chopped

Directions:
1. Rinse the chicken (including the cavity) under cold running water. Pat and dry with the paper towel. Using your fingers, gently lift the skin away from breast meat on each side (to form 2 pockets).

2. Combine butter, dip, basil and garlic in a bowl. Gently push the butter mixture under chicken skin, being careful not to split the skin.
3. Heat the oil in a large frying pan. Add chicken, breast side down. Cook and turn until golden or approximately for 10 minutes. Place a wire rack in the bowl of a 5 liter slow-cooker. Place the chicken on wire rack, breast side up. Season the chicken with salt and pepper. Cover. Turn on the slow-cooker on low. Cook approximately for 4 hrs. or until chicken is tender and cooked through.
4. Serve the chicken with the vegetables.

9. Philly Cheese steak

Ingredients:

1 beef top sirloin steak (1.5 lbs.), cut into thin strips

2 halved and sliced medium green or sweet red peppers

2 halved and sliced medium onions

1 can (14.5 oz.) beef broth (reduced-sodium)

1 envelope of onion soup mix

12 halved slices provolone cheese

6 split hoagie buns

Optional:
Mushrooms

Pickled hot cherry peppers

Directions:

1. In the slow cooker, place the beef, pepper, onions, broth and soup mix, cook on low approximately for 6 hrs. or more.
2. On a cookie sheet, arrange the hoagie buns, spread the Philly cheese steak filling over the buns, cover with cheese and broil until the cheese is melted and it's toasted approximately for 2 minutes or so. If desired, top it with the pickled hot peppers and serve immediately.

10.   Cheese and Shrimp Chowder

Ingredients:

8 ounce shredded Cheddar cheese

3 peeled and diced potatoes

4 tbsp. of dry sherry

1 c. of celery with tops, sliced

1/4 tsp. of pepper

1 chopped onion

4.5 oz. can of un-drained tiny shrimp

1 can of milk, evaporated

Parsley

2 c. of water, boiling

Salt to taste

Directions:

1. In Crockpot, put onion, potatoes, celery and boiling water. Cover; cook on low until potatoes are tender or approximately for 10 to 12 hrs. Stir in evaporated milk, pepper, shrimps and cheese during the last hr.

2. Stir in salt and sherry (just before serving). Sprinkle it with parsley.

11.   Creole Dump Chicken

Ingredients:

4 to 6 chicken pieces (1.5 lbs.)

1 can of whole tomatoes, chopped and un-drained (14 oz.)

1 clove garlic, minced

1/4 c. of green bell pepper

1/2 tsp. of basil, dried

2 tsp. of Worcestershire sauce

1/4 tsp. of pepper sauce (optional)

2 tsp. of red wine vinegar

1 tbsp. of olive oil

1/4 tsp. of pepper

1/4 c. of onion, chopped

1/4 tsp. of salt

Directions:

For freezing:
1. Take a 1-gallon freezer bag and place all of the ingredients into it. Put down the bag flat in the freezer and ensure that the freezer bag is entirely sealed.

To defrost and cook:
1. Pull out the bag from the freezer the night before you plan to cook it. From the freezer, put the bag on the outermost shelf.

For baking:
1. Heat oven to 175 C/350 F. Take a large baking dish and place all of the ingredients into it, turn the chicken to coat. Depending upon the pieces of the chicken that have used, bake approximately for half an hour to an hour or until the chicken juices run clear.

For the Crockpot:
1. Place the chicken in the bottom of the Crockpot and transfer the left over ingredients over the chicken. Cook the chicken on high approximately for 4 to 6 hrs. or on low approximately for 6 to 8 hrs. or until done.

12.   Fisherman Stew

Ingredients:

1 can of tomato sauce (8 oz.)

1 can of tomatoes w/juice, crushed (28-oz)

1 c. of white wine

1 chopped onion

3 minced cloves garlic

3 tbsp. of parsley

1 green pepper, chopped

2 tsp. of basil

1 tsp. of thyme

1/2 tsp. of paprika

1 tsp. of oregano

1/3 c. of olive oil

1/2 tsp. of cayenne pepper

Pepper and salt to taste

1 chopped hot pepper (optional)

Seafood:

1 doz. scallops

1 doz. shrimp

1 doz. clams

1 doz. Mussels

1 cubed whitefish fillet, deboned

Directions:

1. Take a Crockpot and place all of the ingredients (except the seafood). Cook on low approximately for 6 to 8 hrs. Add seafood to the cooked ingredients (About half an hour prior to serving). Turn the Crockpot on high, stir gently for one or two times. Serve the fish with the sourdough bread.

Remember never have the scallops, shrimp, clams or mussels in the freezer, you may also use canned.

13.   Russian Chicken

Ingredients:

2 Packages of Soup Mix (Dry Onion)

16 ounce of Russian Dressing

2/3 c. of Apricot Preserves

Directions:

For freezing:
1. Take a 1-gallon freezer bag and place all of the ingredients into it. Put down the bag flat in the freezer and ensure that the freezer bag is entirely sealed.

If you want to cook immediately:
1. Pre-heat the oven to 175 C/350 F. Take a large baking dish and place all of the ingredients into it, turn the chicken to completely coat. Bake the chicken until the chicken juices run clear (approximately half a hrs. for chicken breasts or for a hrs. for the chicken pieces).

To defrost and cook:
1. Pull out the bag from the freezer the night before you plan to cook it. From the freezer, put the bag on the outermost shelf.
2. Preheat the oven to 175 C/ 350 F. Take a large baking dish and empty the bag's contents into it, bake until the chicken juices run clear (approximately half a hrs. for chicken breasts or for a hrs. for the chicken pieces).

14.   Parisienne Chicken

Ingredients:

6 halves of Chicken Breasts, boneless

Paprika as per the taste

10.75 oz. of Mushroom Soup, condensed cream

½ c. of White Wine, dry

4.5 oz. of Mushrooms, sliced

¼ c. of Flour, all purpose

Pepper & Salt as per the taste

Directions:

1. Sprinkle the chicken with paprika, salt & pepper (as per your taste). Arrange them in the slow cooker.
2. Take a bowl and combine the condensed soup, wine & mushrooms in it. Now, take one more bowl & mix in the sour cream & flour. Stir the mixture of sour cream in the wine & mushrooms. Pour this mixture on chicken. Drizzle some more paprika as per the taste.
3. Cover, cook on low approximately for 6 to 8 hrs.

15.   Potato Chicken

101 Dump Dinner Recipe 19

Ingredients:

8 halves of Chicken Breasts, boneless

1 oz. of Onion Soup. Dry mix

10.75 oz. of Mushroom Soup, condensed cream

4 Potatoes, cubed

1/3 c. of Milk

1 tbsp. of Corn Starch

Directions:

1. Take slow cooker and place the chicken & potatoes in it. Mix in the soup, milk, cornstarch & soup mix. Pour them on chicken & potatoes. Cook all of the ingredients on low approximately for 8 to 10 hrs.

16.   Spicy Chicken Legs

Ingredients:

1.5 c. of Salad Dressing, blue cheese

12 Chicken drumsticks

½ c. of Butter, cubed

5 oz. of Pepper Sauce, red pepper

½ tsp. of Onion Powder

½ tsp. of Garlic Powder

Pepper & Salt as per the taste

Directions:

1. Take a slow cooker and arrange the drumsticks into it. Sprinkle them equally with the butter cubes. Now, pour the sauce over the chicken. Season them with pepper, garlic powder, and salt & onion powder. Cover; cook them on high approximately for 3 hrs.

17. Meatballs

Ingredients:

1 grape jelly's jar (16 oz.)

1 package of meatballs, Italian style

1 jar of chili sauce

Directions:

1. Take a crock pot and dump all of the ingredients into it and set the temperature of the Crockpot to low. The meatballs are already pre-cooked. You may put the meatballs on before work and they would be ready for the dinner.

For added flavor:
1. When adding everything to the Crockpot, you may add a few dashes of hot sauce, 2 tbsp. of lemon juice and 1/2 tsp. of molasses.

18.   Sticky Turkey

Ingredients:

4 turkey legs

3 tbsp. of ketchup

3 tbsp. of peanut butter

1 tbsp. of soy sauce

2 tbsp. of oil

Directions

1. Take a Crockpot and place the turkey legs into it. In a separate bowl, combine the remaining ingredients and spoon them over the turkey legs. Cook on low approximately for 8 to 10 hrs. (meat would be falling off the bones, so delicious and tender).

19.   Teriyaki Dump Chicken

Ingredients:

1.5 lbs. of chicken pieces

1 crushed clove garlic

2 tbsp. of sherry (or rice wine)

1/3 c. of soy sauce

1.5 tbsp. of brown sugar

1.5 tbsp. of cider vinegar

1/2 tbsp. of minced ginger

Directions:

For freezing:
1. Take a 1-gallon freezer bag and place all of the ingredients into it. Put down the bag flat in the freezer and ensure that the freezer bag is entirely sealed.

To defrost and cook:
1. Pull out the bag from the freezer the night before you plan to cook it. From the freezer, put the bag on the outermost shelf.

For baking:
1. Heat oven to 175 C/350 F. Take a large baking dish and place all of the ingredients into it, turn the chicken to coat. Depending upon the pieces of the chicken that have used, bake approximately for half an hour to an hour or until the chicken juices run clear.

For the Crockpot:
1. Place the chicken in the bottom of the Crockpot and transfer the left over ingredients over the chicken. Cook the chicken on high approximately for 4 to 6 hrs. or on low approximately for 6 to 8 hrs. or until done.

20.   Spiced-Citrus Chicken

Ingredients:

1 value-pack chicken

2 tbsp. of paprika

2 tbsp. of lemon juice

2 tbsp. of orange juice

1 tbsp. of lime juice

2 tbsp. of chili powder

1 tbsp. of olive oil

1 tsp. of cayenne

1/4 tsp. of pepper

1/4 tsp. of salt

Directions:
1. Take a Crockpot and place entire value-pack into it (normally around 4 pounds). Blend the remaining ingredients and pour

them over the chicken. Cook on low approximately for 4 to 6 hrs.

2. Serve with a side of rice, making gravy of the salad, veggie or juices on the side

21.   Macho Nacho Chicken

Ingredients:

4-6 chicken breasts

1 small bag of tortilla chips

2 c. of grated cheese, Monterey Jack

1 c. of picante sauce

1/2 c. of guacamole

1/2 c. of sour cream

Directions:

1. In a Crockpot, line the bottom of stoneware with tortilla chips. Arrange the chicken pieces over the top. Pour the picante sauce over the chips and chicken. Cook on low approximately for 8 hrs. and put in the cheese. Cook until the cheese is melted.

2. Remove from the crock pot and top it with guacamole and sour cream.

22.   Tipsy Chicken

Ingredients:

8 Chicken Thighs

1 tbsp. of Flour (All purpose)

10.75 oz. of Mushroom Soup, condensed cream

1 ¼ cup of Chablis Wine

10.75 ounce of Celery Soup, condensed cream

5 oz. of Green Olives, Pimento stuffed

8 oz. of Mushrooms, sliced

Pepper & Salt as per the taste

1 tbsp. of Butter

Directions:

1. Take a skillet and over med. high flame, melt the butter in it and add in the Chicken Thighs. Season them with pepper & salt. Cook them till it become golden brown in color. Now, place the ingredients in the slow cooker and arrange the thighs in it.
2. Reduce the flame to med. Put in both the condensed creams to skillet. Cook them to become creamy. Pour this mixture on the chicken. Add flour, olives, wine & mushrooms.
3. Cover them & cook on low approximately for 8 hrs.

23.   Creole Chicken

Ingredients:

8 Chicken thighs

1 c. of Rice, long grain & uncooked

¼ lbs. of cooked & cubed Ham

1 Bell Pepper, green & chopped

16 oz. Tomatoes

6 oz. of Tomato Paste

6 green & chopped Onions

½ lbs. of Polish Sausage

2 pinch of Pepper Sauce

1 tsp. of Salt

2 c. of Water

Directions:

1. Take a slow cooker and place the chicken, tomatoes, ham, pepper sauce, bell pepper, tomato paste and green onions in it. Cover & cook them on low approximately for 4-5 hrs.

2. Take a saucepan and combine rice & water in it. Bring them to boil. Reduce the flame & cover. Simmer approximately for 15 to 20 mins.

3. Now, mix the sausage & rice in a slow cooker. Cover & cook them on High approximately for 15-20 mins.

24. Chicken & Noodles

Ingredients:

12 oz. of Egg Noodles, frozen

4 halves of Chicken Breasts, boneless

2 Stalks of Celery, well chopped

1 chopped Onion

Pepper & Salt as per the taste

6 c. of Water

Directions:
1. In a slow cooker, place the pepper, onion, chicken, water & salt. Add in the celery as per the requirement. Cook on low approximately for 6 to 8 hrs.
2. When the chicken becomes tender, remove it & chop it to bite size pieces. Keep the chicken aside. Increase the heat of slow cooker to high & put the egg noodles in. Cook till the noodles become tender. Add the chicken to the noodles & season them accordingly.

25. Delicious Chicken

Ingredients:

10.75 oz. of Celery soup, condensed cream

4 halves of Chicken Breasts, boneless

10.75 oz. of Chicken soup, condensed cream

½ c. of Sour Cream

Directions:

1. Take a slow cooker and place the chicken in it. Combine both of the soups in a separate bowl and then pour them over the chicken to coat them well.

2. Cover & cook on Low approximately for 7 to 8 hrs. Now, stir the sour cream in just ½ hrs. before the serving.

26. Super Chicken

Ingredients:

1.5 pounds of Chicken Breasts, boneless

10.75 ounce of Herb & Chicken Soup, condensed cream

½ Onion, red & chopped

4 oz. of Mushrooms

Marsala Wine, a pinch

Directions:

1. Take a slow cooker and combine wine, soup, chicken, onion & mushrooms in it. Cook on low approximately for 3 hrs.

27. Chicken wings

Ingredients:

5.5 lbs. of Chicken Wings

¼ c. of Lemon Juice

1 tsp. of Garlic Powder

¼ c. of Molasses

12 oz. of Chili Sauce

2 tbsp. of Worcestershire Sauce

1 tbsp. of Salsa

2.5 tsp. of Chili Powder

3 pinch of Pepper Sauce

Directions:

1. Take a slow cooker and place the chicken in it. Combine salt, Chile sauce, molasses, lemon juice, Worcestershire sauce, salsa, pepper sauce, chili powder & garlic powder in a bowl. Mix them together & pour the mixture on the chicken.

2. Cook them on med. low approximately for 5 hrs.

28. Slow Cooker Dump and Go Cheesy Chicken

Ingredients

2 cans of Cheddar cheese soup, condensed cream (11 oz.)

6 chicken breast halves, skinless and boneless

1 tsp. of garlic powder

1/2 c. of milk

Pepper and salt to taste

Directions

1. Use cooking spray to spray the slow cooker and add in the chicken breasts. Mix together the milk and soup in a medium bowl and pour the mixture over the chicken. Season the chicken with garlic powder, pepper and salt to taste.

2. Cover and cook on High approximately for 6 hrs. Remember: while cooking, don't pick up the lid.

29. Dump Casserole

Ingredients:

1 lbs. of beef, ground

1 can of tomato sauce (8 oz.)

1 can of corn, cream-style (15 ounce)

1/2 c. of onion, chopped

2 c. of uncooked egg noodles

1 c. of sharp cheddar grated cheese,

1/2 tsp. of chili powder

2 tsp. of Worcestershire sauce

1/4 tsp. of pepper

2 tbsp. of cooking oil

1.5 tsp. of salt

2.5 c. of hot water

Directions:

1. Preheat the oven to 175 C/350 F and brown the ground beef in the oil.

2. Dump in tomato sauce, onion, noodles, hot water, salt, chili powder, pepper, Worcestershire sauce, corn and cheese. Combine them together.

3. Spoon into a baking pan (9-by-13-inch) and bake them until noodles are tender or approximately for 40 to 50 mins.

30. Chinese Pork & Vegetable Hot Pot

Ingredients:

2 (8 oz.) med. white turnips, peeled and cut into wedges (3/4-inch-wide)

2 c. of baby carrots

2 1/4 lbs. of pork shoulder, boneless, trimmed and cut into 1.5 inch chunks

1 can chicken broth, reduced-sodium (14 oz.)

2 to 4 tsp. of Chinese chili-garlic sauce

1 tsp. of aniseed, or 1 star anise pod

1 bunch of sliced scallions, green and white parts separated

1/4 c. of soy sauce, reduced-sodium

2 tbsp. of fresh ginger, minced

3 tbsp. of dry or medium sherry,

1 cinnamon stick

4 minced cloves garlic

1 tbsp. of rice vinegar

4 tsp. of cornstarch mixed with 2 tbsp. of water

4 tsp. of brown sugar

1/2 c. of water

For garnish:

2 tbsp. of sesame seeds, toasted

Directions:

1. Place the turnips and carrots in a larger slow cooker or the bottom and up the sides of a 4-quart. Top it with scallion whites and pork. Bring water, broth, vinegar, sherry, soy sauce, ginger, Chile-garlic sauce (to taste), garlic and brown sugar to a simmer over medium-high heat in a medium saucepan. Pour them over the vegetables and pork. Nestle cinnamon stick and star anise pod into the stew. Cover; cook until the vegetables and pork are tender, on low approximately for 5.5 to 6 hrs. or on high approximately for 3 to 3.5 hrs.

2. Remove the cinnamon stick and star anise pod. From the surface of the stew, blot or skim any fat that is visible. Now, put in the cornstarch mixture, cover; cook on high approximately for 10 to 15 minutes or until slightly thickened (stirring twice or thrice). Serve sprinkled with sesame seeds and scallion greens.

31. Slow-cooker massaman lamb shanks

Ingredients:

1/3 c. of chopped peanuts, roasted and unsalted

650 grams of chat potatoes

4 lamb shanks, trimmed (1.5kg)

3 tsp. of fish sauce

101 Dump Dinner Recipe 34

2 tbsp. of plain flour

1/3 c. of mass man curry paste

1 thinly sliced halved red onion

2/3 c. of pineapple juice

1.5 c. of chicken stock

2 tbsp. of lime juice

1 cinnamon stick

1 can of coconut milk (400ml)

2 tbsp. of olive oil

To serve:

Coriander leaves and Steamed rice,

Directions:

1. Take a large snap-lock bag and place the flour and shanks into it. Season them with pepper and salt. Seal the bag and shake it to coat well. Heat half of the oil over medium-high heat in a large frying pan. Cook the shanks until browned all over or approximately for 4 to 5 mins., if required, you may add more quantity of oil (in batches). Transfer to bowl of a slow cooker and add potatoes to the slow cooker.

2. Heat the left over oil over medium heat in a pan and put in the onions. Cook until softened or approximately for 3 minutes, stirring frequently. Add the paste and cook until fragrant or for an additional minute. Add lime juice, pineapple juice, fish sauce and stock. Bring to the boil.

3. Transfer the mixture to the slow cooker and put in the cinnamon. Cover it with lid. Cook on low approximately for 6 hrs. turning the shanks in middle of the cooking. Add coconut milk and peanuts. Cook approximately until lamb is very tender or for 1 to 1.5 hrs. Serve with coriander and rice.

32.   Italian Beef

Ingredients:

1 ½ pounds beef chuck roast

1 ½ dry Italian salad dressing mix

½ cup water

8 ounce jar Pepperoncini peppers

4 hamburger buns, split

Method:

1. Place the beef chuck roast in the slow cooker.
2. Add the Italian dressing mix.
3. Pour water. Cook on High for 6-7 hours.
4. In the last hour, shred the meat. If you are not able to shred it properly, cook for a longer time.
5. Add the peppers and some of the juice (optional).
6. Serve over the split buns.

33. Sour Cream Roast

Ingredients

1 Tbsp whole allspice berries

½ cup Vinegar

2 cups water

1 onion, chopped

2 Tbsp cornstarch

3 pounds chuck roast beef

1 cup cold whipping cream

3 bay leaf

salt and pepper to taste

Directions

Preheat the oven to 350 F

In a large pot bring to boil salted water. Cook the pasta until well done in about 8 minutes then drain

2 .Sauté the onion and ground beef in a large skillet over medium heat. And in 15 minutes add the spaghetti sauce.

3. Grease a suggested baking dish of 9x13 inch and layer the follows: Provolone cheese, 1/2 sauce mixture, 1/2 of the ziti, sour cream. Top with Parmesan Cheese

Bake for 30 minutes until the cheese is melted

34. Dump Coke

Ingredients:

4 lbs. boneless skinless chicken breasts

1 cup barbecue sauce

1 teaspoon onion powder

1 teaspoon garlic powder

12 ounces Coke

Salt and pepper to taste

Directions:

1. Take a mixing bowl and mix all ingredients in it except chicken. This will give you a mixture.
2) Now take a roasting dish and place chicken in it. Pour mixture on chicken.
3) Preheat oven to 350 F and place dish in it. Cook it in oven for 30 to 45 minutes.
4). Serve and enjoy. This recipe will give you 6 servings in total.

Nutritional facts per serving:

Calories: 400kcal
Carbohydrates: 20g
Protein: 34g
Fat: 20g

Fiber: 1g

35. Lemon Dill "dump" Chicken

Ingredients:

1/4 cup water

3 tablespoons lemon juice

4 boneless skinless chicken breasts

2/3 ounce Seasonings Italian salad dressing mix

1 tablespoon dill weed

1/2 cup oil

Directions:

1) Take a freezer bag and mix all ingredients in it. Now you can freeze this bag and can use this whenever you want to use it.
2) Thaw and allow chicken to marinade.
3) Finally you can cook chicken by baking it or grilling it. Bake it or grill it until chicken is cooked.
4) Serve and enjoy. This recipe will give you 4 servings in total.

Nutritional facts per serving:

Calories: 350kcal
Carbohydrates: 1g
Protein: 25g
Fat: 30g

Fiber: 1g

36. Dump Pepper Lime Chicken

Ingredients:

4 chicken breasts

1/4 teaspoon salt

1 teaspoon basil

1 tablespoon olive oil

1 teaspoon pepper

1/4 cup lime juice

2 minced garlic cloves

1/2 teaspoon lime peel

Directions:

1) Take a freezer bag and combine all ingredients in it. Now marinate it for a night or freeze it and use it whenever you want to cook it.
2) Before cooking if it is frozen then defrost it. Now you can cook it in 2 ways by baking it in oven or cooking it in crockpot.
3) To cook in oven bake for 30 to 45 minutes at 350 F.
4) To cook in crockpot add all ingredients in crockpot and cook on low setting for 4 to 5 hours.
5) Serve and enjoy. This recipe will give you 4 servings.

Nutritional facts per serving:

Calories: 280kcal
Carbohydrates: 3g
Protein: 30g
Fat: 17g
Fiber: 1g

37.   Pineapple dump Chicken

Ingredients:

1 cup pineapple tidbits

2 teaspoons dry mustard

1 cup pineapple preserves

1/2 cup ketchup

1/4 cup butter melted

1/2 cup chopped onion

1/2 lb. chicken piece

Directions:

1)First of all combine all ingredients in the crockpot. Cook it on high setting for 4 to 6 hours or on low setting for 6 to 8 hours. Make sure everything is cooked otherwise cook for some more time. This recipe will give you 6 servings in total.

Nutritional facts per serving:

Calories: 460kcal
Carbohydrates: 70g
Protein: 8g
Fat: 17g
Fiber: 2g

38. Sweet Salsa Dump Chicken

Ingredients:

1 1/4 ounce taco seasoning mix

8 ounces apricot jam

12 ounces salsa

1 1/2 lbs. chicken pieces

Directions:

1) Combine all ingredients and place them in a baking dish.
2) Preheat oven to 350 F and place baking dish in the oven.
3) Bake it until chicken is cooked usually it take 45 minutes to cook completely.
4) For freezing you can combine all ingredients in a freezer bag and can cook whenever you want to cook it after defrosting it.
5) This recipe will give you 4 servings in total.

Nutritional facts per serving:

Calories: 383kcal
Carbohydrates: 42g
Protein: 20g
Fat: 15g
Fiber: 2g

39. Dump Swiss steak

Ingredients:

1 lb. round steak

15 ounce diced tomatoes

1 1/4 ounce beef and onion soup mix

1 1/4 ounce brown gravy mix

Mashed potatoes

Directions:

1) Cut steak in proper portion size and combine it with all other ingredients except potatoes.
2) Place all ingredients in a baking dish and place in oven.
3) Bake it after covering at 350 F for 90 minutes.
4) Now serve it with mashed potatoes.
5) This recipe will give you 2 servings in total.

Nutritional facts per serving:

Calories: 380kcal
Carbohydrates: 20g
Protein: 54g
Fat: 10g

Fiber: 3g

40. Grandma Randolph's Noodles

Ingredients:

4 cups beef broth

2 cups all-purpose flour

1 teaspoon ground black pepper

1 teaspoon salt

4 eggs

Directions:

1) Beat eggs, flour, salt and pepper with the help of beater and make a dough.
2) Make noodles by rolling it and make it 1/4 inch thick.
3) Dry them for 2 hours and then put them in boiling stock and boil.
4) Serve and enjoy.
5) This recipe will give you 6 servings in total.

Nutritional facts per serving:

Calories: 212kcal
Carbohydrates: 32g
Protein: 10g

Fat: 5g
Fiber: 2g

41. Super Quick Dump Pot Roast

Ingredients:

3 -4 lbs. chuck roast

2 cups water

1/2 cup ketchup

2 sliced garlic cloves

1 lb. carrot peeled and sliced

1 1/4 ounce onion soup mix

1 extra-large onion sliced

Directions:

1) First of all rinse beef. Add ½ vegetables and garlic in the crockpot.
2) Place beef over vegetables. Now place remaining vegetables over beef. Pour onion soup mix on it.
3) Add 2 cups of water and ketchup in the crockpot.
4) Now time to cook it for 8 hours on low heat.
5) Serve and enjoy. This recipe will give you 6 servings in total.

Nutritional facts per serving:

Calories: 600kcal
Carbohydrates: 15g
Protein: 42g
Fat: 44g
Fiber: 3g

42. Teriyaki Chicken Crockpot

Ingredients:

16 ounce carrots

1 red onion

20 ounce can pineapple (do not drain it)

1 cup teriyaki sauce

4 chicken breasts

4 garlic cloves

Directions:

1) First of all chop all vegetables and mince garlic.
2) Add half vegetables and pineapple in the crockpot and place chicken above them. Now put remaining half vegetables and pineapple over chicken.
3) Pour teriyaki sauce over all ingredients.
4) Close the crockpot and cook it on low heat for 8 hours.

5) Serve and enjoy. This recipe will give you servings in total

Nutritional facts per serving:

Calories: 510kcal
Carbohydrates: 62g
Protein: 37g
Fat: 14g
Fiber: 7g

43. Dump It in Meatloaf

Ingredients:

2 1/2 lbs. ground beef

2 cups breadcrumbs

4 large eggs

1/3 cup dried parsley

2 tablespoons basil

3/4 cup milk

1 tablespoon lemon pepper

2 teaspoons sea salt

10 3/4 ounce cream of celery soup

2 teaspoons minced garlic

3/4 cup cheddar cheese

Directions:

1) Preheat oven to 375 F degrees. In a big mixing bowl mix all ingredients very well.
2) Now spread all this mixture in a baking dish. Make sure baking dish should not be greasy and mixture should be moist enough.
3) Now place dish in the preheated oven for baking.
4) Bake it in oven unless it becomes brown from top and cooked completely.
5) Serve after slicing it. This recipe will give you 12 servings in total.

Nutritional facts per serving:

Calories: 350kcal
Carbohydrates: 15g
Protein: 24g
Fat: 20g
Fiber: 1g

44. Lemon Garlic Dump Chicken

Ingredients:

1 1/2 lbs. chicken pieces

1/8 teaspoon pepper

3 tablespoons lemon juice

2 tablespoons chopped parsley

4 tablespoons olive oil

2 chopped garlic cloves

Directions:

1) Preheat oven to 350 F degrees.
2) Take large size baking dish and place all ingredients in it. Make sure that the chicken is coated with all other ingredients in the baking dish.
3) Now bake it until chicken is completely cooked. Normally it takes 40 to 60 minutes to complete cooking of chicken.
4) Serve and enjoy. This recipe will give you 6 servings in total.

Nutritional facts per serving:

Calories: 350kcal
Carbohydrates: 2g
Protein: 20g
Fat: 29g
Fiber: 0g

45. Pineapple-Honey lamb chops

Ingredients:

6 -8 thick boneless lamb chops

6 ounce frozen pineapple concentrate, thawed

1/2 cup tarragon vinegar

6 1/4 ounce parmesan and butter rice mix

1/3 cup honey

1/4 cup packed brown sugar

Directions:

1) First of all make chops brown by cooking the in very little oil and then transfer them into crockpot but before it make crockpot little greasy by cooking spray.
2) Take a mixing bowl and mix all other ingredients in it to make a mixture.
3) Pour this mixture on meat in crock pot and close the crockpot.
4) Cook at low setting for 5 to 6 hours.
5) Serve and enjoy. This recipe will give you 6 servings in total.

Nutritional facts per serving:

Calories: 440kcal
Carbohydrates: 37g
Protein: 40g
Fat: 12g
Fiber: 0g

46. Fruity Crock Pot Chicken

Ingredients:

1 large sliced onion

6 boneless skinless chicken breasts

1/3 cup orange juice

Hot cooked rice

1/2 cup dried apricot, chopped

1/3 cup cherries

2 chopped garlic cloves

1 tablespoon grated orange zest

2 tablespoons Dijon mustard

2 tablespoon soy sauce

2 tablespoon Worcestershire sauce

Directions:

1) In the bottom of crockpot place onions. Place chicken on top of onion layer.
2) Take a big mixing bowl and mix all remaining ingredients in it to make a mixture.
3) Pour this mixture on top of chicken.
4) Close the crockpot and cook on low setting for 8 hours.
5) Serve and enjoy. This recipe will give you 6 servings in total.

Nutritional facts per serving:

Calories: 180kcal
Carbohydrates: 13g
Protein: 28g
Fat: 2g
Fiber: 2g

47. Apricot Chicken

Ingredients:

3 lbs. skinless chicken pieces

1 1/2 ounce dry onion soup mix

1/2 cup French dressing

1/2 cup apricot jam

Directions:

1) Take a big mixing bowl and mix soup mix, French dressing and jam in it. Place chicken in the crockpot and pour prepared mixture in the crockpot. Mix chicken and mixture very well.
2) Close the crockpot and cook on low setting for 6 to 8 hours.
3) Serve and enjoy. This recipe will give you 6 servings in total.

Nutritional facts per serving:

Calories: 440kcal
Carbohydrates: 37g
Protein: 32g
Fat: 18g
Fiber: 1g

48. Shredded Beef Burritos

Ingredients:

1/2 teaspoon paprika

1/2 teaspoon ground cumin

2 lbs. chuck roast

1 teaspoon dry oregano

1/2 teaspoon red pepper flakes

2 cups chopped tomatoes

1/2 cup chopped chili pepper

1 chopped onion

I minced garlic clove

1 cup water

12 flour tortillas

Directions:

1) First of all place roast in the crockpot and add all remaining ingredients over roast except tortillas
2) Close crockpot and cook on low setting for 8 to 10 hours.
3) Now time to shred roast with the help of a knife or fork in the crockpot. After shredding mix all ingredients very well.
4) Finally drain it and serve with flour tortillas.
5) Serve and enjoy. This recipe will give you 6 servings in total.

Nutritional facts per serving:

Calories: 590kcal
Carbohydrates: 35g
Protein: 33g
Fat: 34g
Fiber: 3g

49.   Machaca Beef

Ingredients:

1 1/2 lbs. lean beef roast

1 large sliced onion

4 ounce can chopped green beans

2 low sodium beef bouillon cubes

1 1/2 teaspoons dry mustard

1/4 teaspoon garlic powder

3/4 teaspoon seasoning salt

1/2 teaspoon black pepper

1 cup salsa

Directions:

1) Put all ingredients in the crockpot except salsa and mix them well. Add water now that should cover all ingredients in the crockpot.
2) Close the crockpot and cook all these on low setting for 10 to 12 hours or unless meat becomes tender.
3) Drain meat and save liquid to use later in the recipe.
4) Now it is time to shred beef with the help of forks. After shredding mix salsa, meat and reserved liquid.
5) Finally serve it and enjoy.

Nutritional facts per serving:

Calories: 86kcal
Carbohydrates: 3g
Protein: 33g
Fat: 3g
Fiber: 1g

50. Cube Steak and Gravy

Ingredients:

2 lbs. cube steaks

Salt and pepper to taste

1 ounce onion gravy mix

10 1/2 ounce cream of mushroom soup

2 cups water

Flour

Directions:

1) Season steak with salt and pepper and then use flour for dredging.
2) In a saucepan fry it and then put in to crockpot. Add remaining ingredients in the crockpot and lock it.
3) Now cook on low setting for 6 to 8 hours.
4) You can serve it with rice. This recipe will give you 4 servings in total.

Nutritional facts per serving:

Calories: 63kcal
Carbohydrates: 5g
Protein: 3g
Fat: 3g
Fiber: 0g

51. Beef Stroganoff

Ingredients:

6 cups hot cooked noodles or cooked rice

8 ounce container sour cream

8 ounce container cream cheese

1/4 teaspoon pepper

8 ounce can sliced mushrooms

1 can condensed cream of onion soup

1 can condensed cream of mushroom soup

1 large chopped onion

2 lbs. beef stew meat

Directions:

1) Pour all ingredients in the crockpot and mix them very well except sour cream and cheese. Mix these ingredients in crockpot very well.
2) Close crockpot and cook on low setting for 8 to 10 hours unless beef is tender.
3) Now add cream cheese and sour cream in crockpot and cook unless it melts.
4) Now serve it with rice or noodles.
5) This recipe will give you 6 servings in total.

Nutritional facts per serving:

Calories: 600kcal
Carbohydrates: 42g
Protein: 44g
Fat: 30g
Fiber: 3g

52. Honey Glazed "dump" Chicken

Ingredients:

1/4 cup melted butter

1/8 cup soy sauce

1/2 cup honey

1 1/2 lbs. chicken pieces

Directions:

1) In a baking dish place chicken with all other ingredients and coat chicken with them.
2) Preheat oven to 350 F degrees. Place baking dish in the preheated oven and cook until chicken is cooked. This will take almost 1 hour to cook completely but if you are using chicken breast pieces then it will take less time to cook.
3) Serve and enjoy. This recipe will give you 4 servings in total.

Nutritional facts per serving:

Calories: 450kcal
Carbohydrates: 32g
Protein: 20g
Fat: 27g
Fiber: 1g

53. Thunderbird Roast

Ingredients:

2 lbs. chuck roast

1 (1 ounce) package dry onion soup mix

1 (3/4 ounce) package brown gravy mix

1 1/2 cups apple juice

Directions:

1) Add roast in the crockpot and pour all other ingredients over roast. Cover it and cook on low setting for 5 to 8 hours.
2) Serve and enjoy. This recipe will give you 4 servings in total.

Nutritional facts per serving:

Calories: 400kcal
Carbohydrates: 18g
Protein: 50g
Fat: 14g
Fiber: 1g

54. Turkey Breast

Ingredients:

3 1/2 lbs. boneless turkey breast

14 ounce chicken broth

2 tablespoons melted butter

3 tablespoons Worcestershire sauce

1 teaspoon thyme

Directions:

1) Wash turkey and then dry it with paper towel. Place turkey in the crockpot and pour chicken broth over turkey.
2) Now cook on low setting for 2 hours and then add remaining ingredients in it.
3) After adding remaining ingredients cook again on low setting for 8 hours.
4) Now serve and enjoy. This recipe will give you 4 servings in total.

Nutritional facts per serving:

Calories: 700kcal
Carbohydrates: 3g
Protein: 90g
Fat: 11g
Fiber: 0g

55. Slow Cooker Taco Soup

Ingredients:

½ pound ground beef

1 medium onion, chopped

½ can (½ a 16 ounce can) chili beans, with liquid

½ can (½ a 15 ounce can) kidney beans with liquid

½ can (½ a 15 ounce) can whole kernel corn, with liquid

½ (½ a 8 ounce) can tomato sauce

1 cup water

(14.5 ounce) can tomatoes, peeled, diced

½ can (2 ounce) green chili peppers, diced

½   package taco seasoning mix

½ cup Cheddar cheese, shredded

Sour cream to garnish

Method:

1. Place a skillet over medium heat. Add ground beef.
2. Cook until browned. Drain and keep aside
3. Place the ground beef in a slow cooker.
4. Add onions, chili beans, kidney beans, corn, tomato sauce, water and tomatoes.
5. Also add the green chili peppers and taco seasoning mix. Mix well.
6. Set the slow cooker on Low and cook for 8 hours.
7. Serve topped with cheddar cheese and sour cream.

56.   Crunch Cherry Dump Cake

Ingredients:

1/2 cup melted butter

18 ounce white cake mix

21 ounce cherry pie filling

Lemon juice

Directions:

1).We will use 9x13 size pan in this recipe.
2) Make pan a little greasy with the help of cooking spray and spread filling in the pan.
3) Take a mixing bowl and mix melted butter and cake mix in the mixing bowl very well.
4) Pour this mixture over filling in the pan.
5) Now time to bake it in the oven. Place it in the oven and bake it for 1 hour at 325 degrees F.
6) Cool down it for a few minutes and then serve to enjoy.
7) This recipe will give you 12 servings in total.

Nutritional facts per serving:

Calories: 300kcal
Carbohydrates: 47g
Protein: 2g
Fat: 12g
Fiber: 1g

57. Fruit Dump Cake

Ingredients:

29 ounce can pumpkin

12 ounce can evaporated milk

1 cup sugar

1/4 teaspoon pumpkin pie spice

1/2 teaspoon ground cinnamon

1 cup butter

1 cup pecans

18 ounce yellow cake mix

3 eggs

Directions:

1) We will use 9x13 size pan in this recipe.
2) In a mixing bowl mix pumpkin, evaporated milk, spices, sugar and eggs very well and make a mixture. Pour it into pan and add cake mix over it.
3) Pour melted butter on cake mix.
4) Now time to bake it in the oven. Place it in the oven and bake it for 1 hour on 350 degrees F.
5) Serve and enjoy. This recipe will give you 20 servings in total.

Nutritional facts per serving:

Calories: 310kcal
Carbohydrates: 35g
Protein: 4g
Fat: 17g
Fiber: 1g

58. Pumpkin Dump Cake

Ingredients:

32 ounce can peaches in heavy syrup

1/2 cup butter

18 1/4 ounce yellow cake mix

Ground cinnamon

Directions:

1) First of all preheat oven to 375 degrees F.
2) Add peaches in a 9x13 size pan and then sprinkle dry cake mix over peaches in the pan.
3) Melt butter and then sprinkle it over the cake mix. Add cinnamon to the butter.
4) Finally it is time to bake it. Place it in preheated oven and bake it for 45 minutes.
5) Serve it and enjoy. This recipe will give you 10 servings in total.

Nutritional facts per serving:

Calories: 370kcal
Carbohydrates: 50g
Protein: 3g
Fat: 15g
Fiber: 2g

59. Peach Cobbler Dump Cake

Ingredients:

32 ounce can peaches in heavy syrup

1/2 cup butter

18 1/4 ounce yellow cake mix

Ground cinnamon

Directions:

1) First of all preheat oven to 375 degrees F.
2) Add peaches in a 9x13 size pan and then sprinkle dry cake mix over peaches in the pan.
3) Melt butter and then sprinkle it over the cake mix. Add cinnamon to the butter.
4) Finally it is time to bake it. Place it in preheated oven and bake it for 45 minutes.
5) Serve it and enjoy. This recipe will give you 10 servings in total.

Nutritional facts per serving:

Calories: 370kcal
Carbohydrates: 50g
Protein: 3g
Fat: 15g
Fiber: 2g

60. Blueberry Dump Cake

Ingredients:

1 package yellow lemon cake mix

1/2 cup

1/2-1 cup walnut pieces

2 cups blueberries

1 1/2 cups crushed pineapple

Directions:

1) In a 13 x 9-inch pan make ayes of pineapple and blueberries. Sprinkle cake mix over layers of fruits. Now pour melted butter over cake mix.
2) Finally add the nuts on top of all ingredients.
3) Now bake it at 375 degrees F for 40 to 60 minutes.
4) Serve and enjoy. This recipe will give you 12 servings in total.

Nutritional facts per serving:

Calories: 312kcal
Carbohydrates: 40g
Protein: 3g
Fat: 16g
Fiber: 2g

61. Black Forest Dump Cake

Ingredients:

18 1/2 ounce chocolate cake mix

21 ounce can cherry pie filling

3 1/2 ounce vanilla instant pudding mix

1 cup flacked coconut

20 ounce can crushed pineapple

Directions:

1)Take a 9 x 13 inch pan and make 3 layers in it, first layer of pineapple, second layer of coconut and third layer of dry pudding mix
2)Now add cherry pie filling in the pan and finally sprinkle cake mix over it.

3) Melt butter and pour it over all other ingredients.
4) Now bake it on 350 degrees F for 60 minutes.
5) Serve it after cooling it down. This recipe will give you 6 servings in total.

Nutritional facts per serving:

Calories: 500kcal
Carbohydrates: 70g
Protein: 7g
Fat: 36g
Fiber: 10g

62.   Three-Fruit Dump Cake

Ingredients:

21 ounce can apple pie filling

15 1/4 ounce can sliced pears drained

5 1/4 ounce can peaches, sliced, drained

9 ounce package yellow cake mix

1/4 cup butter

Directions:

1) Take an 8"x8 inch size baking dish and make it greasy by cooking spray.
2) Preheat oven at 350 degrees F.
3) In a big mixing bowl mix pie filling, pears and peaches. Pour this mixture in the baking dish evenly. Add cake mix over this mixture.
4) Pour melted butter over cake mix and then place pan in the preheated oven for baking.
5) Bake it for 45 to 60 minutes in the oven and then serve it.
6) This recipe will give you 8 servings in total.

Nutritional facts per serving:

Calories: 315kcal
Carbohydrates: 50g
Protein: 3g
Fat: 10g
Fiber: 4g

63. Beef Fajitas

Servings per Recipe: 6 servings
Cooking Time: 8-10 hours

Ingredients:

12 pieces 7-inch flour tortillas

8-oz can stewed tomatoes

¼ tsp. salt

1 garlic clove, minced

1 tsp. coriander

1 tsp. cumin

1 tsp. chili powder

½ tbsp. parsley

1 to 2 jalapeno peppers

1 bell pepper, cut into ½-inch pieces

1 onion chopped

1 ½ lbs. flank steak

2 tsps. lime juice

Optional Ingredients:

Salsa

Sour cream

Guacamole

Shredded Monterey Jack cheese

Shredded Colby cheese

Directions:

1) Trim steak fat and slice into 12 pieces. In crockpot, mix salt, garlic, coriander, cumin, chili powder, parsley, jalapeno pepper, bell pepper, onion and steak.
2) Pour in undrained tomatoes and set crockpot at low settings and cook for 8 to 10 hours.
3) After 8 or 10 hours of cooking, remove steak and shred. Return shredded meat, mix and add lemon juice. Stir well.
4) Just before serving dinner, toast tortillas to desired hotness or crispiness.
5) To assemble, place 1/12 of beef fajitas into each tortilla top with salsa, guacamole, cheese and sour cream or as desired.
6) Serve and enjoy.

64. Beef Stroganoff

Servings per Recipe: 6 servings
Cooking Time: 7 hours

Ingredients:

1 pkg egg noodles

1 8-oz container of sour cream at room temperature

1 ½ tbsps. cornstarch

1 12-oz can ginger ale

1 10.75-oz can Cream of Mushroom Soup

1 pkg onion soup mix

1 can mushrooms, drained

2 lbs. Stew meat, sliced into ½-inch cubes

2 tbsps. water

Directions:

1) In crockpot, dump all ingredients except for egg noodles, cornstarch and water.
2) Set on low settings, cook stroganoff for 6 hours.
3) On the 6th hour, mix well water and cornstarch. Pour into pot of beef, mix and continue cooking for another hour or a half on high settings.
4) When nearly done, cook egg noodles following manufacturer's instructions and drain well.

5) To serve, divide egg noodles on to 6 plates and top with 1/6 of beef mixture, serve and enjoy.

65. Pot Roast

Servings per Recipe: 12 servings
Cooking Time: 8 – 9 hours

Ingredients:

5 ½ pounds pot roast

1 ¼ cups water

1 1-oz package dry onion soup mix

2 10.75-oz cans condensed cream of mushroom soup

Directions:

1) Mix water, dry onion soup mix and cream of mushroom in slow cooker.
2) Add pot roast in the slow cooker and coat with soup mixture.
3) Cover and cook for 8 to 9 hours on low setting.
4) Serve with a slice of bread or a cup of rice.

66. Ham and Broccoli Casserole

Servings per Recipe: 4 servings
Cooking Time: 3 ½ - 4 hours

Ingredients:

8-oz Velveeta cheese spread

1 cup uncooked instant rice

2 cups broccoli florets

1 cup diced ham or any leftover meat

1 cup milk

1 can (10.75-oz) condensed cream of mushroom soup

Directions:

1) Whisk together milk and mushroom soup in slow cooker until well combined.
2) Add cheese, rice, broccoli, and ham or leftover meat. Mix well.
3) Cook on low settings for 3 ½ hours. Check if rice is cooked to desired doneness and soup is to desired thickness, if not continue cooking for another 30 minutes.
4) Equally pour into 4 serving bowls, serve and enjoy.

67. Shrimp and Cheese Chowder

Servings per Recipe: 4 servings
Cooking Time: 10 – 12 hours

Ingredients:

2 tbsps. parsley, chopped

Salt to taste

4 tbsps. dry sherry

4-½ oz. can tiny shrimp, undrained

8-oz Cheddar cheese, shredded

1 can evaporated milk

¼ tsp. pepper

2 cups boiling water

1 onion, chopped

1 cup sliced celery with tops

3 potatoes, peeled and diced

Directions:

1) In crockpot, dump in boiling water, onion, celery and potatoes.
2) Cook on low settings for at least 10 hours, until potatoes are tender.
3) At the 9th or 11th hour, dump in shrimps, cheese, evaporated milk and pepper. Stir to mix well. Cover and cook for another hour.

4) Once done, stir in salt and sherry. Adjust salt and pepper to taste.
5) Transfer into a serving bowl and garnish with chopped parsley.
6) Serve and enjoy.

68.   Italian Style Eggplant

Servings per Recipe: 4 servings
Cooking Time: 4.5 – 5 hours

Ingredients:

Pepper and salt to taste

1 tsp. dried oregano or basil

1 tbsp. capers, drained

1 tbsp. sugar

2 tbsps. balsamic vinegar

½ cup pitted ripe olives, cut in half

3 tbsps. tomato sauce

1 16-oz can diced tomatoes, undrained

1 tbsp. olive oil

2 ribs celery, cut into 1-inch pieces

2 medium onions, sliced thinly

1 ¼ lbs. eggplant, cut into 1-inch cubes

Directions:
1) In slow cooker, dump in tomato sauce, tomatoes, oil, celery, onions and eggplant.
2) Cook for at least 3.5 to 4 hours at low settings, until eggplant is tender.
3) When eggplant is tender, dump in oregano, capers, sugar, vinegar and olives. Stir to mix well.
4) Season with pepper and salt to taste. Cover and continue cooking for another hour.
5) To serve, transfer eggplant into a serving dish and enjoy.

69.   Beef Roast Sandwich with Au Jus Dip

Servings per Recipe: 10 servings
Cooking Time: 10 – 12 hours

Ingredients:

20 slices French bread

1 tsp. garlic powder

1 tsp. dried thyme

1 tsp. dried rosemary crushed

3 whole black peppercorns

1 bay leaf

1 beef bouillon cube

½ cup soy sauce

4 lbs. boneless beef roast

Directions:

1) Trim fat from beef roast and place in slow cooker.
2) Mix well in a medium bowl garlic powder, thyme, rosemary, peppercorns, bay leaf, bouillon, and soy sauce. Pour over beef in slow cooker and add water to cover beef with liquid.
3) Cook roast beef on low settings for 10 to 12 hours or to desired tenderness.
4) To serve, remove meat from slow cooker and shred. Evenly distribute shredded meat onto sliced bread and serve with au jus from the liquid in the slow cooker.

70. Meat Loaf

Servings per Recipe: 8 servings
Cooking Time: 8 hours

Ingredients:

¼ cup brown sugar

1 tsp. yellow mustard

1 ½ cup ketchup, divided

1 cup Ritz cracker crumbs

2 egg

1 ½ tsp. salt

½ cup onions, chopped

½ cup green peppers, chopped

2 lbs. ground beef

Directions:

1) Mix well ¾ cups ketchup, cracker crumbs, salt, eggs, onion, and green pepper and ground beef in a medium bowl. It is best to use hands to mix the Pattie well. Once thoroughly combined, form mixture into a loaf.
2) Spray all sides of slow cooker with cooking spray. Then, line your slow cooker with foil from bottom to sides and spray once more with cooking spray.
3) Place loaf of meat on top of foil and cook on low settings for 6 to 8 hours or until meat is cooked thoroughly.
4) Once meat is cooked, mix together in a medium bowl brown sugar, mustard and remaining ketchup. Then spread on top of meat loaf and continue cooking for another 15 minutes.
5) When done, remove meat loaf and let it stand for at least 10 minutes before slicing and serving.

71. Chicken Teriyaki

Servings per Recipe: 6 servings

Cooking Time: 6 to 8 hours

Ingredients:

1 ½ lbs. chicken piece

½ tbsps. minced ginger

1 ½ tbsps. brown sugar

1 ½ tbsps. cider vinegar

2 tbsps. rice wine

1/3 cup soy sauce

1 clove garlic, crushed

Directions:

1) You can prepare this food ahead of time by placing all ingredients in a re-sealable bag then putting inside the freezer. When needed, just defrost in the microwave for 1.5 pounds.
2) Just place all ingredients inside a crockpot, set crockpot on low setting and cook for 6 to 8 hours. If you want this dish to cook quicker, then put crockpot on high settings and cook for around 4 to 5 hours.
3) When done, serve right away and enjoy.

72. Goulash

Servings per Recipe: 8 servings

Cooking Time: 10 hours and 15 minutes

Ingredients:

2 tbsps. flour

1 cup water

½ tsp. dry mustard

2 tsps. paprika

2 tsps. salt

1 tbsp. brown sugar

2 tbsps. Worcestershire sauce

½ cup ketchup

1 clove garlic, minced

1 large onion, sliced

2 lbs. stew meat, cut into 1-inch cubes

Directions:

1) Place cubed meat inside crockpot and top with sliced onions.
2) Pour inside crockpot water, mustard, paprika, salt, sugar, Worcestershire sauce, ketchup and garlic. Stir to mix well.
3) On low settings, cook for 9 to 10 hours.
4) When goulash is cooked, mix 1 tbsp. cold water with 2 tbsps. flour. Mix well until no lumps is seen then pour into crockpot.
5) Increase settings to high and mix well. Allow to cook for another 15 minutes to let sauce thicken.
6) When sauce has thickened, turn off crockpot, serve and enjoy while hot.

73. Cuban Beans

Ingredients:

½ pound black beans, dried

1 cup water

1 cup vegetable broth

½ cup red bell pepper, chopped

½ cup green bell pepper, chopped

½ cup yellow bell pepper, chopped

1 tablespoon olive oil

¾ teaspoon salt or to taste

1 teaspoon fennel seeds, crushed

1 teaspoon coriander, powdered

1 teaspoon cumin, powdered

1 teaspoon dried oregano

1 tablespoon sherry or red wine vinegar

1 can (10 ounce) tomatoes, diced

2-3 green chilies, chopped

To Serve:

2 ½ cups hot cooked rice

Hot sauce (optional)

Method:

1. Clean the beans. Wash well with water. Soak the beans in water. Water should be at least 3 inches above the beans. Cover and keep aside overnight.
2. Drain and place the beans in a slow cooker. Add water, fennel seeds, vegetable broth, all the bell peppers, olive oil, salt, coriander powder, cumin powder and oregano.
3. Cover. Set on High and cook for 5 hours or until the beans are tender.
4. When the beans are tender add vinegar and tomatoes. Stir well.
5. To serve, place over hot cooked rice and serve with hot sauce.

74. Potato and Ham Casserole

Servings per Recipe: 4 servings
Cooking Time: 5 – 6 hours

Ingredients:

1 6-oz package, herb-seasoned stuffing mix

¼ cup butter, melted

2 cups cooked chopped ham or leftover meat

2 cups grated cheddar cheese

1 10.75-oz can reduced fat cream of chicken soup

1 8-oz container sour cream

1 tsp. salt

1 tbsp. dried minced onion

1 30-oz package frozen hash brown potatoes, cubed or shredded

Directions:

1) Grease bottom and sides of slow cooker with cooking spray.
2) In greased slow cooker, mix ham, cheese, cream of chicken soup, sour cream, salt, dried onion and hash browns.
3) On top of hash brown mixture, sprinkle evenly the stuffing mix and then drizzle butter all over.
4) Cook on low settings for 5 to 6 hours or until casserole is set. If in a hurry, you can cook on high for 2 to 4 hours.

75. Beans and Corn Chicken Dinner

Servings per Recipe: 3 servings
Cooking Time: 6 hours

Ingredients:

1 can mexi-corn

1 can black beans, drained and rinsed

2 cans Ro-Tel, Drained

1 package Tyson individually frozen Southwest Pepper Trio Chicken

Directions:

1) Grease crockpot with cooking spray and dump in black beans, Ro-tel and Mexi-corn.
2) Stir to mix ingredients well.
3) Add Chicken on top of the mixture and cook on low settings for 6 hours.
4) When done, remove from pot, serve and enjoy.

76. Mixed Vegetable Curry

Ingredients:

2 carrots, medium sized, sliced

1 potato, cut into ½ inch cubes

½ can (7.5 ounce) chick peas, drained, rinsed

4 ounces fresh beans, stringed , cut into 1 inch pieces

½ cup onion, coarsely chopped

2 cloves garlic, minced

1 tablespoon quick cooking tapioca

1 teaspoon curry powder

¼ teaspoon red chili flakes

Salt to taste

½ teaspoon coriander, powdered

1 big pinch cinnamon powder

7 ounce vegetable broth

½ can (7 ¼ ounce) tomatoes (do not drain), chopped

Hot cooked rice

Method:

1. Add carrots, potatoes, onions, chickpeas, green beans, tapioca, garlic, coriander, chili flakes, salt and cinnamon.
2. Pour the vegetable broth over it.
3. Cover. Set on Low and cook for 7-9 hours or on High for 3 ½ to 4 hours
4. Add the tomatoes along with the liquid. Stir well.
5. Keep covered for 5 minutes.
6. Serve over hot rice.

77. Meatballs with Sweet and Sour Sauce

Ingredients:

1 egg

1 1/2 cups water

1 cup packed brown sugar

1 onion, diced

1 pound ground beef

3 tablespoons soy sauce

3 tablespoons all-purpose flour

1/4 cup dry bread crumbs

1/4 cup distilled white vinegar

Directions

1. Combine bread crumbs, ground beef, onions and egg. Thoroughly mix and form it like a golf size balls.
2. In a medium fry the meatballs in a large skillet and set aside.
3. Combine the flour white vinegar brown sugar and soy sauce. Thoroughly mix all the sauce ingredients. Then add the meatballs. Let it simmer and stir it as often as you could for a minute or 3.

78. Chicken Adobo

Servings per Recipe: 6 servings
Cooking Time: 6 to 10 hours

Ingredients:

1 whole chicken, around 3 lbs., cut into pieces

½ cup vinegar

¾ cup low sodium soy sauce

8 cloves garlic crushed

1 small sweet onion, diced

1 tbsp. peppercorns

2 bay leaves

Directions:

1) Grease slow cooker with cooking spray.
2) Place onions, peppercorns, garlic and bay leaves at the bottom of the pot. Place chicken pieces on top and pour in seasoning.
3) Cook for 6 to 8 hours or until chicken is cooked through. If you want tender chicken, you can cook up to 8 to 10 hours on low settings with ½ cup additional water.
4) Once cooked, chicken adobo is best paired with a cup of rice.

79. Barbecued Pot Roast

Servings per Recipe: 6 servings
Cooking Time: 8 to 10 hours

Ingredients:

1 tsp. Worcestershire sauce

1 onion, chopped

24 peppercorns

½ cup tomato paste

1 tsp. salt

2 lbs. pot roast

¼ cup sugar

¼ cup water

Directions:

1) Place pot roast into crockpot and season with salt all over.
2) Pour tomato paste all over pot roast and embed peppercorns all over it too.
3) Add Worcestershire sauce, onions and water into crockpot and mix.
4) Sprinkle sugar all over pot roast and cook on low settings for 8 to 10 hours.
5) Serve pot roast with accumulated sauce. It is best paired with a hoagie or your favorite garden salad.

80. Chicken Cacciatore

Servings per Recipe: 6 servings
Cooking Time: 7 to 9 hours

Ingredients:

2 tbsps. minced garlic

1 large onion, finely diced

3 large tomatoes, diced

1 tsp. paprika

1 tsp. salt

1 tsp. freshly crushed pepper

6 skinless, boneless chicken breast halves

3 medium carrots, peeled and cut into 2-inch lengths

2 medium potatoes, peeled and cut into 2-inch lengths

1 medium green bell pepper, seeded and cut into 2-inch lengths

1 tbsp. olive oil

½ cup water

Directions:

1) Set crockpot to high and heat oil. Sauté garlic for 5 minutes or until lightly browned. Add onions and sauté for another 5 to 10 minutes or until soft and translucent. Add tomatoes and continue sautéing for another 5 minutes.
2) Place chicken on top of onion-tomato mixture. Season chicken with paprika, pepper and salt. Place potatoes and carrots on top of chicken. Then top potatoes with bell pepper. Pour water all over.
3) Reset crockpot settings to low and cook for 7 to 9 hours or until chicken is cooked to desired tenderness.
4) Transfer to a serving platter and enjoy.

81. Dump Chicken Caribbean Style

Servings per Recipe: 6 servings
Cooking Time: 6 to 8 hours

Ingredients:

1 ½ lbs. chicken piece

½ cup golden raisins

1/3 cup orange juice

½ tsp. nutmeg

¼ cup brown sugar

8-oz pineapple chunks in juice

Directions:

1) Dump all ingredients inside a crockpot and cook on low settings for 6 to 8 hours or until chicken is cooked and desired chicken tenderness is reached.
2) This dish can also be prepared in advance. Just combine all ingredients in a zipper lock bag and place in the freezer for future use. Make sure that you store chicken flattened and in a single layer for easy crockpot cooking. If this is not possible, then you may need to defrost chicken in the microwave prior to placing in the crockpot. Once ready for cooking, just remove chicken and marinade from bag, place in the crockpot and follow cooking instructions from step 1.

82. Vegetable and Beef Soup

101 Dump Dinner Recipe 90

Servings per Recipe: 6 servings
Cooking Time: 6 hours

Ingredients:

Pepper and salt to taste

1 1.25-oz package beef with onion soup mix

1 28-oz can crushed tomatoes

1 15-oz can sliced potatoes with juice

1 15-oz can carrots with juice

1 15-oz cans green beans

1 15.25-oz cans whole kernel corn, undrained

1 lb. cubed beef stew meat

1 cup water

Directions:

1) In slow cooker, dump in water, soup mix, tomatoes, potatoes, carrots, green beans, corn and meat.
2) Season with pepper and salt.
3) Cook dish on low settings for 6 hours.
4) Once nearly done, taste and adjust seasoning.
5) Remove from pot and transfer to a serving bowl, serve and enjoy.

83. Shrimp and Cheese Chowder

Servings per Recipe: 4 servings
Cooking Time: 10 to 12 hours

Ingredients:

Parsley

Salt to taste

4 tbsps. dry sherry

4.5 oz. can tiny shrimp, undrained

8 oz. Cheddar cheese, shredded

1 can evaporated milk

¼ tsp. pepper

2 cups boiling water

1 onion, chopped

1 cup sliced celery with tops

3 potatoes, peeled and diced

Directions:

1) In crockpot, dump in boiling water, onion, celery and potatoes. Cook for 10 to 11 hours on low settings or until potatoes are very tender.
2) Once potatoes are tender, stir in shrimps, cheese, evaporated milk and pepper. Continue cooking for another hour.
3) Once cooking is done, turn off crockpot and stir in salt and sherry. Adjust seasoning to taste.

4) To serve, pour soup equally on to 4 serving bowls, garnish with parsley, serve and enjoy.

84. Chicken with Sweet Salsa

Servings per Recipe: 5 servings
Cooking Time: 30 minutes

Ingredients:

1 ½ lbs. chicken piece, around 5 pieces

12 oz. salsa

8 oz. apricot jam

1 1.25-oz package taco seasoning mix

Directions:

1) This is a great recipe that does not make use of a crockpot. However, it is still a dump dinner recipe because all you need to do is dump all ingredients in a greased rectangular baking dish.
2) Pop the dish into a preheated 350ºF oven and bake for 45 to 60 minutes or until chicken is cooked and juices run clear. Then, serve and enjoy.
3) This dish can also be prepared ahead of time and stored in a zip lock bag in the freezer. So, what you need to do is

place all ingredients in a re-sealable bag, lay it flat in the freezer and remove the night before cooking. Then, just follow cooking instructions above.

85. Clam Chowder

Servings per Recipe: 8 servings
Cooking Time: 8 hours

Ingredients:

1 pint heavy whipping cream

1 quart half and half cream

2 6.5-oz cans minced clams

1 10.75-oz can New England clam chowder

1 10.75-oz can condensed cream of potato soup

1 10.75-oz can condensed cream of celery soup

Directions:

1) In slow cooker, dump in half and half cream, 1 can undrained clams, clam chowder, cream of potato soup and celery soup.
2) Cook on low settings for 5 to 7 hours. Then an hour before your desired dinner time, mix in heavy whipping cream and cook of another hour.

3) Once cooking is done, turn off crockpot, evenly pour chowder into 8 bowls, serve and enjoy.

86. Chicken Taco Soup

Servings per Recipe: 8 servings
Cooking Time: 7 hours

Ingredients:

Crushed tortilla chips, optional

Sour cream, optional

Shredded cheddar cheese, optional

3 whole skinless, boneless chicken breasts

1 1.25-oz package taco seasoning

2 10-oz cans diced tomatoes with green chilies, undrained

1 12-fluid oz. can or bottle of beer

1 8-oz can tomato sauce

1 15-oz can whole kernel corn, drained

1 15-oz can black beans

1 16-oz can chili beans

1 onion, chopped

Directions:
1) Set slow cooker to low settings.

2) In slow cooker, mix diced tomatoes, beer, tomato sauce, corn, black beans, chili beans and onions. Pour in taco seasoning, stir to blend well. Then place chicken on top of the mixture, then press chicken breasts down firmly to submerge it and be covered by the other ingredients.
3) Cook for five hours. Then remove chicken breasts and let it cool for at least 15 minutes so it will be easy to handle. Once chicken is cool to touch, shred chicken.
4) Return shredded chicken to pot, stir to combine and continue cooking for another 2 hours.
5) To serve this dish, evenly ladle into 8 bowls, top with a dollop of sour cream, garnished with Cheddar cheese and crushed tortilla chips and enjoy.

87. Chicken and Shrimp Jambalaya

Servings per Recipe: 8 servings
Cooking Time: 7 hours

Ingredients:

1 tbsp. hot sauce

2 tbsps. chopped fresh flat leaf parsley

1 lb. medium shrimp, peeled and deveined

2 3.5-oz bags boil-in-bag long grain rice

1 14-oz can fat-free, lower sodium chicken broth

2 14.5-oz cans diced tomatoes with onion and green peppers, undrained

¼ tsp. Spanish smoked paprika

½ tsp. dried thyme

2 tsps. salt-free Cajun seasoning

4 oz. turkey kielbasa, halved and cut into ¼-inch thick slices

2 garlic cloves, minced

1 cup chopped celery

1 cup chopped green bell pepper

2 cups chopped onion

¾ lb. skinless, boneless chicken thighs, cut into 1-inch pieces

1 tbsp. canola oil

Directions:
1) Set slow cooker on high and heat oil. Add garlic, celery, bell pepper and onions. Allow to sauté for 10 minutes.
2) Dump in chicken, chicken broth, diced tomatoes, paprika, thyme, Cajun seasoning and turkey kielbasa. Lower slow cooker settings to slow and cook for 6 hours.
3) Before the sixth hour is up, cook rice according to manufacturer's instructions and upon six hours of slow cooking, add rice into slow cooker. Mix in hot sauce, shrimp and parsley.
4) Increase slow cooker settings to high and cook for an additional 20 minutes.
5) To serve, transfer equally into bowls and garnish with parsley, serve and enjoy.

88. Curried Pork over Rice

Servings per Recipe: 6 servings
Cooking Time: 7 – 9 hours

Ingredients:

Cilantro sprigs, optional

3 cups hot cooked basmati rice

½ cup coconut milk

2 garlic cloves, minced

1 tsp. ground cumin

1 tsp. Madras curry powder

1 ½ tsps. salt

1 tbsp. minced peeled fresh ginger

2 tbsps. tomato paste

1 tbsp. sugar

2 tbsps. all-purpose flour

¼ cup fat-free, lower-sodium chicken broth

1 cup chopped red bell pepper

1 cup chopped onion

3 ½ cups cubed red potato

1 ½ lbs. boneless pork loin, cut into 1-inch cubes

1 tsp. canola oil

Directions:

1) Set slow cooker to high and heat oil. Add pork and cook for at least 30 minutes per side.
2) Then add garlic, cumin, curry powder, salt, ginger, tomato paste, sugar, flour, chicken broth, bell pepper, and onion. Mix well until flour is dissolved thoroughly. Add in potatoes.
3) Lower crockpot settings to low and cook until potatoes are tender. Around 6 to 8 hours.
4) When potatoes are tender, stir in coconut milk. Cook on high for 15 minutes or until coconut is heated through.
5) Serve with a cup of rice and enjoy.

89. Char Siew Pork

Servings per Recipe: 8 servings
Cooking Time: 8hours and 30 minutes

Ingredients:

½ cup fat free, low sodium chicken broth

1 2lb boneless pork shoulder, trimmed

½ tsp. five spice powder

1 tsp. dark sesame oil

2 tsps. grated peeled fresh ginger

2 tsps. minced garlic

3 tbsps. honey

3 tbsps. ketchup

¼ cup hoisin sauce

¼ cup low sodium soy sauce

Directions:

1) The night before cooking time, place pork in a re-sealable bag. Then in a small bowl, whisk well five spice powder, sesame oil, ginger, garlic, honey, ketchup, hoisin sauce and soy sauce. Pour inside re-sealable plastic with pork and place in the ref to marinate. You can marinate for at least 2 hours or overnight.
2) The next day, pour all contents of the re-sealable bag into the crockpot and on low settings cook for 8 hours.
3) Remove pork and place in a bowl and shred with two forks.
4) Meanwhile, add chicken broth into crockpot and cook on high until sauce has thickened. This takes around 30 minutes.
5) Serve shredded pork with sauce on the side.

90. Roast Turkey Mediterranean Style

Servings per Recipe: 8 servings
Cooking Time: 8 hours

Ingredients:

Thyme sprigs, optional

3 tbsps. all-purpose flour

½ cup fat-free, low sodium chicken broth, divided

1 4-lb boneless turkey breast, trimmed

¼ tsp. freshly ground black pepper

½ tsp. salt

1 tsp. Greek seasoning mix

1 ½ tsps. minced garlic

2 tbsps. fresh lemon juice

½ cup oil-packed, sun-dried tomato halves, julienned

½ cup pitted Kalamata olives

2 cups chopped onion

Directions:

1) In slow cooker, dump turkey breast, salt, Greek seasoning mix, garlic, lemon juice, julienned tomatoes, olives and onions.
2) Pour in ¼ cup of chicken broth and on low settings cook for 7 hours.
3) Once the 7 hours is nearly up, whisk together in a small bowl flour and ¼ cup broth. Pour into crockpot and mix well.
4) Continue cooking for another 30 minutes.
5) To serve, slice turkey into ¼-inch thick slices, place on a platter and serve.

91. Flaxseed Oatmeal

Servings per Recipe: 1
Calories per Serving: 374

Ingredients:

1 tbsp. molasses

1 tbsp. flaxseeds

¼ tsp. ground nutmeg

½ tsp. ground cinnamon

1 tsp. ground ginger

¼ cup dried, unsweetened cherries

½ cup old-fashioned oats

1 cup water

Directions:

1) On medium high fire, place a small sauce pan and heat nutmeg, cinnamon, ginger, cherries, oats and water.
2) Bring to a boil, once boiling reduce fire and simmer for five minutes.
3) Once sticky and cooked, turn off fire, add flaxseeds, cover and let it stand for five minutes more.
4) Drizzle with molasses, serve and enjoy.

92. Oysters

Servings per Recipe: 4
Calories per Serving: 80

Ingredients:

24 medium oysters

2 lemons

Tabasco sauce

Directions:

1) If you are a newbie when it comes to eating oysters, then I suggest that you blanch the oysters before eating.
2) For some, eating oysters raw is a great way to enjoy this dish because of the consistency and juiciness of raw oysters. Plus, adding lemon juice prior to eating the raw oyster's cooks it a bit.
3) So, to blanch oysters, bring a big pot of water to a rolling boil. Add oysters in batches of 6-10 pieces. Leave on boiling pot of water between 3-5 minutes and remove oysters right away.
4) To eat oysters, squeeze lemon juice on oyster on shell, add Tabasco as desired and eat.

93.   Kale Chips

Servings per Recipe: 8
Calories per Serving: 190

Ingredients:

2 tbsps. filtered water

½ tsp. sea salt

1 tbsp. raw honey

2 tbsps. nutritional yeast

1 lemon, juiced

1 cup sweet potato, grated

1 cup fresh cashews, soaked 2 hours

2 bunches green curly kale, washed, ribs and stems removed, leaves torn into bite sized pieces

Directions:

1) Prepare a baking sheet by covering with an unbleached parchment paper. Preheat oven to 150°F.
2) In a large mixing bowl, place kale.
3) In a food processor, process remaining ingredients until smooth. Pour over kale.
4) With your hands, coat kale with marinade.
5) Evenly spread kale onto parchment paper and pop in the oven. Dehydrate for 2 hours and turn leaves after the first hour of baking.
6) Remove from oven; let it cool completely before serving.

94. Beef and Vegetable Soup

Ingredients:

1 ½ pound beef chuck roast

¼ cup barley

1 bay leaf

1 tablespoon oil

2 carrots, chopped

2 stalks celery, chopped

1 small onion, chopped

½ package(8 ounce) frozen mixed vegetables

2 cups water

2 beef bouillon cubes

½ tablespoon white sugar

Black pepper, powdered, to taste

½ can (14 ounce) stewed tomatoes, chopped

salt to taste

Method:

1. Place the chuck roast in the slow cooker.
2. Set the cooker on High and cook for 4-5 hours.
3. During the last hour, add barley and bay leaf.

4. Strain the meat. Throw away the bay leaf. Keep aside the strained liquid and barley.
5. Chop the meat into bite sized pieces.
6. Heat oil in a pot. Add carrots, celery, onion and frozen vegetables. Sauté over a medium heat until the vegetables are tender.
7. Add water, beef bouillon cubes, stewed tomatoes sugar, salt and pepper.
8. Add the strained liquid, beef pieces and barley.
9. When it starts boiling, reduce heat and simmer for 15-20 minutes.

95. Lentil Soup

Ingredients:

2 brown onions , finely chopped

4 sticks celery, trimmed, chopped coarsely

2 carrots, peeled, coarsely chopped

2 cloves garlic, crushed

2 Swede, peeled, chopped coarsely

1 cup red lentils

4 cans tomatoes, diced

4 cups vegetable stock

6 teaspoons cumin, powdered

2 baguette (French loaf), sliced thinly diagonally

200 grams goat cheese

½ cup freshly chopped chives

Method:

1. In a slow cooker add onion, Swede, garlic, carrots, lentil, tomato, stock and cumin powder.
2. Cover. Set on High and cook for 3 hours or the vegetables are tender and the lentil is cooked well.
3. In a small bowl, add goat cheese and chives. Mix well.
4. Meanwhile, preheat a grill. Place the sliced baguette on the baking tray. Place the baking tray on the grill. Grill the loaf for 2 minutes or until the sides are golden.
5. Spread the cheese-chive mixture on the loaf slices. Serve hot with piping hot soup.

96. Pumpkin Soup

Ingredients:

1 ½ medium sized butternut pumpkin, peeled, deseeded, chopped

4 potatoes, medium sized, chopped

2 onions, chopped

3 teaspoons mild curry powder

Salt to taste

Crushed pepper to taste

5 cups vegetable stock

2 cups full cream

½ teaspoon chili powder or to taste

Method:

1. Place in the slow cooker the pumpkin, onions, curry powder and stock.
2. Add salt and pepper.
3. Cover. Set on Low and cook for 5-6 hours or until the vegetables are tender.
4. When tender, switch off the heat. Keep aside to cool.
5. When cooled, transfer into the food processor and blend. Alternately you can use a stick blender. Blend until you get a smooth consistency
6. Add the cream and chili powder. Blend again.
7. Pour the soup into a saucepan and heat it to serve.

97. Pepperoncini Beef

Ingredients:

1 ½ pound beef chuck roast

2 cloves garlic, sliced

½ jar (8 ounce) Pepperoncini

4 hoagie rolls, split lengthwise

8 slices provolone cheese

Method:

1. Make small slits in the roast.
2. Insert the garlic slices in the slits.
3. Place the roast in a slow cooker. Add the Pepperoncini along with the liquid over the meat.
4. Cover. Set on Low and cook for 6-8 hours.
5. When you make sandwiches, place meat in rolls along with the Pepperoncini and top with cheese.
6. Microwave for a few seconds until the cheese is just melted

98. Cinnamon And Apple With Oats

Ingredients:

4 apples, peeled, cored, diced

3 cups coconut milk

3 cups water

2 cup steel cut oats

2 tablespoon brown sugar or to taste

2 tablespoon coconut oil

2 teaspoons cinnamon

½ teaspoon salt or to taste

Method:

1. Spray oil inside the slow cooker thoroughly.
2. Add all the ingredients in the slow cooker.
3. Set on Low and cook for 5-7 hours. (You can do a trial sometime during the take to see how long it takes to cook)
4. Serve with topping of your choice.

99. Breakfast Quinoa

Ingredients:

2 cups quinoa

6 cups milk (normal or almond milk)

8 dates, deseeded, chopped

½ cup pepitas (pumpkin seeds)

2 apples , peeled, cored, diced

4 teaspoon cinnamon powder

½ teaspoon nutmeg powder

2 teaspoons vanilla extract

½ teaspoon salt or to taste

Method:

1. Place all the ingredients in the slow cooker.
2. Set the slow cooker on High and cook for 2 hours or until all the liquid is absorbed OR cook on Low for 8 hours.
3. Refrigerate the unused quinoa. It can last for a week.

100. Spinach and Mushroom Quiche

Ingredients:

3 ½ cups frozen spinach

4 slices bacon

1 tablespoon olive oil

2 cups button mushrooms, chopped coarsely

½ cup red bell pepper, chopped

1 ½ cups Swiss cheese or any other cheese, shredded

8 eggs

2 cups whole milk

2 tablespoons fresh chives, snipped

Salt to taste

Pepper to taste

½ cup packaged biscuit mix

1 disposable slow cooker liner

Cooking spray

Method:

1. Line the slow cooker with the disposable cooker.
2. Spray thoroughly with cooking spray.
3. Squeeze the excess liquid from the spinach and keep aside.
4. Heat a skillet, add bacon. Cook until nice and crispy.
5. Drain it. Crumble the bacon and keep aside.
6. In the same skillet, add olive oil. Heat over medium flame.
7. Add mushroom and bell pepper. Sauté until tender.
8. Add spinach and cheese.
9. Meanwhile, in a bowl add eggs, milk, chives, salt and pepper. Mix well.
10. Pour the egg mixture into the spinach mixture.
11. Gently mix the biscuit mix. Remove from heat.
12. Pour this mixture into the lined slow cooker.
13. Sprinkle bacon on top.
14. Cover. Set the slow cooker on Low and cook for 4-5 hours or on High for 2-2 ½ hours. Insert a knife to check. If it comes out clean then your dish is ready else heat for some more time.
15. Cool for 15-20 minutes before serving.

101. Cranberry Punch

Ingredients:

Juice of 1 orange, keep the peels aside

4 cinnamon sticks, 1 inch each

4 cloves

4 whole all spice

16 ounce cranberry juice

5 ¾ ounce frozen white grape and raspberry concentrate

2 cups water

Method:

1. Remove the pith of the orange peel and make into strips.
2. Make a spice bag with a cotton cheese cloth of about 6 square inches. Keep the orange peel in it along with cinnamon, cloves and all spice in the cheese cloth bag. Bring all the 4 corners together and fasten it with a string.
3. Pour water, cranberry juice, the grape juice concentrate, orange juice and spice bag in the slow cooker.
4. Set the cooker on Low for 5-6 hours of High for 2-2 ½ hours. Discard the spice bag. Serve immediately.

Conclusion

We live in a day and age where everybody is constantly on the move and finding time to provide a tasty, healthy meal has always been a challenge. But no matter how hectic your day is or has been, it's important that you take a breath and enjoy a good, hearty "dump and go" dish by cooking up a delectable meal from one of the simple recipes that I have provided to you. These meals can be enjoyed all year round, however, they're especially tasty during these cold winter months. There's no better way to warm up than with a freshly made "dump and go" and a good book.

Did You Like 101 Dump Dinner Recipes?

Before you go, we'd like to say "thank you" for purchasing our book. So a big thanks for downloading this book and reading all the way to the end. Now we'd like ask for a *small* favor. Could you please take a minute or two and leave a review for this book on Amazon

This feedback will help us continue to write the kind of Kindle books that help you get results. And if you loved it, then please let me know

Leave a review for this book on Amazon by searching the title; **Dump Dinners 101 Fast, Healthy and Easy Dump Dinner Recipes for Everyone!**

Check Out My Other Books

Below you'll find some of my other popular books that are popular on Amazon and Kindle as well. Simply click on the links below to check them out. Alternatively, you can visit my author page on Amazon to see other work done by me.

amazon.com/author/jjlewis

[101 Pork Chop Recipes: Extraordinary and Delicious Pork Chop Recipes for Everyday Meals](#)

[101 Chicken Recipes: A Mouth-Watering Healthy and Delicious Chicken Recipes that will fill your Stomach](#)

[101 Vegetarian Recipes: Top Vegan Diet Recipes to Live a Healthy Lifestyle](#)

[The Juice Cleanse: 101 Healthy Juicing Recipes for Weight Loss](#)

[Diabetes Diet: 101 Healthy Diabetes Recipes to Reverse Diabetes Forever and Enjoy Healthy Living for Life](#)

[Low Fat Recipes: 101 Incredible Quick & Easy Recipes for a Low Fat Diet](#)

[Gluten Free Diet: 101 Delectable and Healthy Gluten-Free Recipes for better lifestyle](#)

[Paleo Diet for Kids: A Fun Pack of 101 Flavorful and Energy-Boosting Paleo Recipes Best In Shaping Healthier, Stronger and Happier Paleo-Nourished Kids](#)

[Mediterranean Slow Cooker: 101 Best of Easy and Delicious Mediterranean Slow Cooker Recipes to a Healthy Life](#)

[Slow Cooker Recipes: The Best of 101 Nutritious and Delicious Healthy Slow-Cooking Recipes for your Crock Pot](#)

[Pressure Cooker Recipes: 101 Mouthwatering, Delicious, Easy and Healthy Pressure Cooker Recipes for Breakfast, Lunch, Dinner in 30 Minutes or Less!](#)

[Wheat Belly Diet: 101 Days of Grain Free Recipes for an Optimum Belly Diet and Weight Loss](#)

[Fast Metabolism Diet Recipes: 101 Best of Metabolism Boosting Recipes to Lose Weight Fast](#)

You can simply search for these titles on the Amazon website to find them.

Want more Bestseller Cook Books for FREE?

Join my **V.I.P** Reading List where I give away **Healthy** and Delicious Recipes FOR **FREE!**

Yes, you heard me right! COMPLETELY FREE to everyone just for being a loyal reader of mine!

http://www.mritchi.com/freecookbook

Made in the USA
Middletown, DE
20 August 2015